Jean Nouvel

Jean Nouvel

Architecture and Design 1976-1995

A Lecture in Italy

Edited by Giampiero Bosoni

EDITORE

Translation
Francisca Garvie

Cover
Foreshortened view
over the park from
inside the Palace
of Congress in Tours, 1993
Photo by Philippe Ruault

Photographs
Gabriele Basilico
Giampiero Bosoni
DR
Georges Fessy
Gaston
Philippe Ruault
Deidi von Schaewen
Jérome Schlomoff
Dahliette Sucheyre
Simonetta Venosta

This book contains the transcript
of Jean Nouvel's first conference
in Italy, held in the Sala d'Onore
of the Palazzo della Triennale in
Milan on 8 April 1995. The
conference was introduced by
the architect Pietro Derossi,
whom we thank for his
participation.

We thank the board of
governors of the Triennale, its
chairman Pierantonino Berté and
its director-general Saverio
Monno for their participation
and support at the conference.
We also thank Olivier Boissière
and Charlotte Kruk of the Studio
Nouvel for their cooperation.

The Jean Nouvel conference and
the transcript of his lecture were
made possible thanks to the
contribution of Unifor.

Distributed outside North, Central
and South America and Italy by
Thames and Hudson Ltd., London

Contents

Jean Nouvel the architect and especially Jean Nouvel the public figure, charismatic and at ease with the media, always provokes very conflicting reactions, especially in Italy. He has enthusiastic admirers who follow him about like a film star and see him as a model of the architect-demiurge of our times, putting the complexity of contemporary life to creative and professional use. He also has detractors who cannot stand him. Some find him inconsistent in terms of what they see as the fundamental principles of the design process. Others recognize his undoubted talent but reject him, or even worse ignore him, as a man of ideas, as a theorist and more generally, on that basis, as an architect with a capital A. Others again rather envy him all his experience, in particular his prestige and the number of projects he has carried out, and subject Nouvel, like many other international architects, to the kind of nauseating and vulgar slander typical of certain blinkered architectural circles in Italy today.

Certainly Nouvel often appears to have characteristics that are not easy to reconcile with a certain image of the architect as intellectual, often based on a kind of fake understatement, that we tend to applaud.

However, the very fact that he arouses such interest

and provokes such conflicting reactions seems to be a positive and useful sign in face of the stagnant and dull debate heard in recent times in Italian and in particular Milanese architectural circles.

So, aside from certain accents typical of his character, it must be said that Nouvel does contribute ideas to the architectural debate (real debate, involving ideas, proposals and verifications, and not the presumptuous and academic debate we sometimes hear) and, even more importantly, experiments with them.

Thanks in part to the importance of the venue, the Sala d'Onore of the Palazzo della Triennale, and to the large audience of about a thousand people who listened attentively—hardly surprising considering Jean Nouvel's charisma—what was intended as an ordinary conference turned into a genuine lecture addressed to Italy, and in particular Milan.

This was indeed the first time Nouvel had appeared before the Italian architectural world at such a major public meeting. It became clear that Nouvel himself took on a certain responsibility for this event from the fact that the day before the conference, by which time it was clear that public expectations were high, he urgently requested further slides to be sent from Paris in order to widen and deepen the spectrum of the debate.

Those who had already seen him at other international public occasions felt that this was one of his most balanced statements, in its measured tone, in the clarity of the theoretical premises and in the detailed and if a little didactic manner in which he discussed a large part of his architectural research.

This was a real lecture, such as is rarely heard in university halls. Of course it was a little theatrical, but at the same time it was authoritative and sound in its theoretical structure and development. In that sense it was quite different from some of those culturally depressing publicity fairs, where the conference turns into a kind of showpiece, that were staged in the same Palazzo della Triennale a few months later involving, as involuntary accomplices, other highly respected architects of international repute.

Although some people only see Jean Nouvel as something of a braggart, his lecture in the Triennale palazzo on 8 April 1995 was certainly one of the most incisive, provocative and stimulating statements ever made in the rather defensive and uncertain world of Italian design.

Regardless, therefore, of whether or not we endorse some of the results of his research, we regard Nouvel's lecture as a point of reference that can inspire further critical reflection and proposals on the cultural, professional and political situation of architecture in particular but also of design in the wider sense in Italy.

Giampiero Bosoni

I am often presented as an architect of "French high tech." I would like to begin by explaining what I mean by the term modernity:

– Modernity is alive, it is not some historical movement that was interrupted a few decades ago.

– Modernity is making the best use of our memory and moving ahead as fast as we can in terms of development.

That is why although I recognize that what is called the "high tech" movement occupied an important place in the seventies, I think that if we entered a new building today and our main impression was "oh what a lovely beam!," that building would be conveying a weak message.

Technique must serve an emotion or a symbol. In today's modernity, what takes priority is the aesthetic of the miracle. That is to say we require maximum performance but at the same time have no desire to know how it is achieved. Everything is becoming increasingly simple and increasingly complex, increasingly light and increasingly compact. Everything is being miniaturized, mechanized. In the field of computers, miniaturization now happens on an incredible scale and at an incredible speed. Materials and techniques are evolving at a spectacular rate. Glass is one example: at the press of a button a sheet of glass can become translucent, opaque, coloured! Soon we will be able to create energy by the passage of light through glass, which means for us architects that we will be able to heat precisely those areas where the heat loss used to be greatest! All this is a matter of technique, but of technique to be used in a natural way.

This century has indeed seen amazing technical developments and man has been fascinated by what the machine can do. One of the first to examine the relationship between machines and architecture was Le Corbusier, which only goes to show that this fascination with the aesthetic of the machine is not new. And it was only logical for the Archigram group to transform it into a poetry of the machine by extrapolating the technical aesthetic of this century. But modernity is alive. It has shifted towards other areas that have little to do with the expression of structural truth. All these buildings that look like carapaces, the high tech buildings that reflect this approach, must today be regarded as the architectural expression of an era, as historical architecture, in the same way as we regard the flowering of technology in the 19th century.

So much for my approach to technique. I use state-of-the art techniques when I find it useful. But as I have often said, it would never occur to me to write a book using only the words invented in the last twenty years. I think it is more interesting to show the relationship between new elements of vocabulary and older, more archaic words as a means of imbuing them with their full meaning, their synergy, their dynamism.

In that sense my architecture may be described as modern and contemporary. I have already rejected the high tech label. I also refuse to be called post-modern insofar as that term has historicist connotations in architecture and nothing horrifies me more than some of the architecture of the past twenty or thirty years, which is nothing but reproduction, the product of a bad academic approach that recycled old forms without knowing how to do so and thereby weakened its own models.

The historical town, the town one loves and which can be read like a book of stone, is made up of successive strata of modernity. We cannot refuse to add our own. It is indeed our responsibility to continue constructing it. We cannot economize with the culture of an era.

For me, the question of the relationship between architecture and design is a question of limits, of boundaries and of the links that can exist between disciplines.

There are fundamental differences between architecture and design. The first is the fact that architecture is unique and can only be specific, whereas design is the creation of multiples aimed at a multitude of individuals. The second is that architecture must convey a sense of the present; it will be up to future generations and the buildings that will be constructed around them whether or not it remains meaningful. In the case of design, the reverse is true: design will be situated in different contexts, surrounded by objects unknown to it. It will pass down through decades, centuries even, and be regarded as the trace of one culture among many. The environment changes: in both cases we see the evidence and the petrification of a form of culture. In the case of architecture, the object is static. In the case of design, the object moves in space and time.

There is a kind of contradiction or paradox in my case: I do not draw as an architect or as a designer. Or very rarely so. I often draw a parallel between the architect and the film producer for I believe their situations are similar. They both have to produce objects by teamwork. They have to enter into a reality which is that of their time, whatever the constraints.

There is a kind of compromise here which the artist, in the strict sense of the term, be he composer, painter or writer, does not have to face.

The architect is concerned with what is real. I approach this reality by using words, concepts and of course from time to time a few scrawls. But I do not do so through drawing or what I would call the intuition of the pencil. Whether a project is architecture or design, it develops through "brain storms," exchanges, objective argument and external analysis. I believe in this need for more profound analysis.

Moreover, in the case of design we are not condemned to re-design everything. Some objects do not lend themselves to being re-designed. Either because techniques have not evolved or because methods, customs and attitudes have not evolved. The designer does not have to systematically renew objects. Conversely, the moment new techniques, new materials, new methods, new attitudes, new programmes appear, the designer is there. And sometimes new environments linked to architectural frameworks are there too.

I will now comment on some of my projects and try to

pose the question of the relationship between architecture and design. I do not presume to answer it in full. I myself came to design by chance and by necessity. By chance because for some of the buildings I constructed I was also asked to design an armchair, a bed or a storage unit. And by necessity because it sometimes happened that for a given space I could not find the object that would enable me to reply to the question it put.

Dolls' House (1983)

This is not a tool box. It is a dolls' house, the smallest project I have ever undertaken. I made it in the late seventies for a review which had organized a competition in a somewhat historicist and nostalgic spirit. I replied that nostalgia would no longer be what it was and that memory and modernity are not a contradiction in terms. I have often paraphrased Borges in saying that I make architecture as seriously as a child who plays. It is this awareness and this serious intent that I have put into this project. Architecture and design often mean recovering sensations and emotions linked to time and living experience. On the basis of an aesthetic of the shop window or grocery, I placed a number of little Proustian *madeleine* biscuits in this box, little mementos full of emotion. The pencils, marbles, varnished wood and red leather are personal mementos but I know that they also reflect experiences common to or shared by certain generations and certain cultures. Architecture and design can draw on them.

Internal view of part of the Dolls' House, showing some of the mementos, 1983

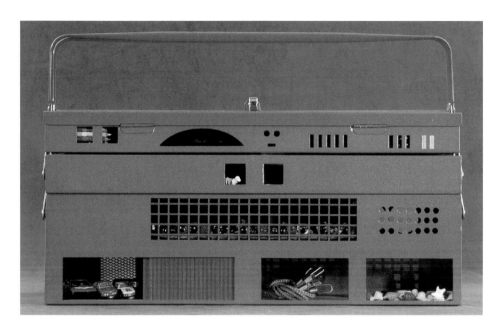

Front view of the Dolls'
House, 1983

Clinic at Bezons (1976)

This private hospital, the extension of a clinic in the Paris suburbs, is the first building that made my name known. Seen in relation to the Pompidou Centre, of which it is a contemporary, it put the question how to express modernity.

It is a rigorously smooth building, covered in the profiled metal sheeting used for trains such as the Trans-Europe Express. It does not expose its structure at all: not a single beam, no structural system. The spectator may wonder how it holds up.

This is a kind of aesthetic of surprise: a building which is not even an extension of the existing building has appeared in this rather sad piece of suburb. It plays on contrast and tends to express a kind of unorthodox modernity.

Detail of a facade of the Bezons clinic, 1976

I use the term unorthodox because I refuse to regard architecture as an autonomous discipline. Merely to know the history of architecture is not enough if you want to write the next pages. By its nature architecture is the production of images. It is influenced by all the images that have been produced, just as the images around us are imprinted on us in the photographic sense of the term. Sometimes we recover them unconsciously. But the architect is a professional observer and must be conscious of the images he uses. The Bezons clinic tries to convey the idea of travel, hence the aesthetic of the hotel room which I developed with the idea of introducing a little poetry into a hospital that all too often merely reflects its own function.

Detail of a facade of the Bezons
clinic, 1976

Lego House (1985)

Another competition, this time organized by Lego: "Your ideal Home." Here too the responses varied, from an Italian castle to a neo-classical villa with little columns. I thought up a disused off-shore oil platform being towed along in the Mediterranean. That is my dream of an extraordinary loft somewhere along the Italian coast.

Overall view of the Lego brick model, 1985
Right: close-up view of the Lego brick model for the "Your ideal Home" competition organized by Lego, which Jean Nouvel interpreted as an off-shore oil platform, 1985

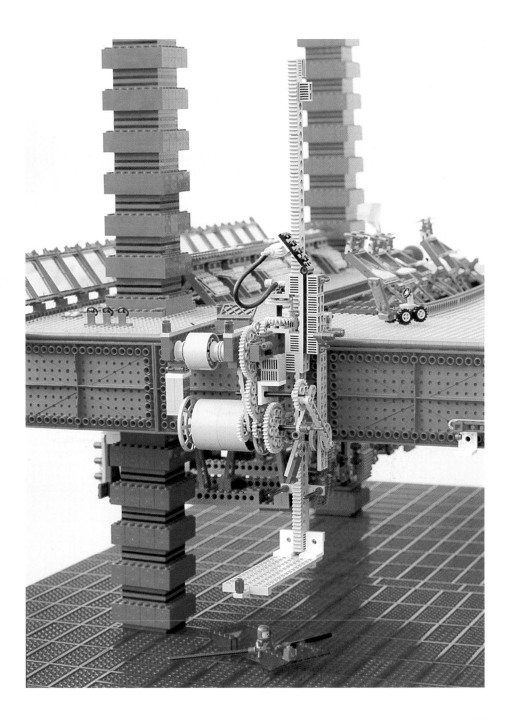

Via (1987)

Another expression of the dream of the tool-box inspired by the director of a large design studio who asked me to think outside any kind of programmatic terms. I opted for a range of furniture in aluminium, a material that is light, can be moulded and is easy to work. We made prototypes: one for a simple 80 × 100 cm box, another for telescopic shelving, which is held in tension between two walls between 3.5 and 5 meters apart. There was also a table based on variable geometry: low, narrow or long, a portfolio table that folds back rather subtly. This *carte blanche* for Via did not lead to the production of an edition. But I do not despair of seeing an edition of this furniture one day.

Container to be used as a tool-box, Via design, 1987

Telescopic shelving units,
shown open and closed,
Via design, 1987

Inox (1992)

The idea was to design a travelling cultural unit, a kind of bus that could take exhibitions, radio broadcasts or meetings to the villages of a French department. I opted for a lorry trailer that unfolds and opens up so that it can be placed on any site. Inside and outside, the lorry has luminous, winking indicators. It is a kind of travelling messenger of culture and information.

Day-time view of the Inox messenger bus, 1992

Night view of the Inox
messenger bus, 1992

The Austerlitz "Bagarre" (1991)

Another form of nomadic or ephemeral architecture: as architect of the Paris Biennale I spent fifteen years working with an extraordinary man, the art critic Georges Boudaille. When he died we decided to pay tribute to him in a "little biennale" held in the parking lot of Austerlitz station. I placed a series of boxes there, consisting of a light-weight structure covered in black tarpaulin, each box marked in yellow with the name of the artist "inhabiting" it. The boundaries of the site and the traffic flow are marked out exactly using the coloured signs of the highway code.

Detail of one of the small
pavilions covered in black
tarpaulin for use by the
Austerlitz "Bagarre" artists,
1991

Nemausus (1985)

Functional markings form part of my visual world. All the Nemausus housing I built in Nîmes reflected my resolve to change the spirit of council housing. At the same time it is simply part of a more global theoretic approach: to develop council housing in a radical manner. For example by introducing large bathrooms with windows. But mainly by substantially increasing the surface area: a beautiful room is a large room. A beautiful flat is a large flat. In Nîmes I did my utmost to achieve this and we managed to create housing that provided 40 percent more than the standard surface area, with all the flats facing two ways and fitted with large, loading-bay doors opening up entirely onto terraces. The whole thing was designed with great attention to detail and to light, so important in southern architecture: the old story of creating shade can be told with materials other than stone and reliefs other than cornices. Inside, we used materials regarded as poor grade (galvanized sheet metal, raw concrete), and which have been upgraded and enhanced by the way François Seigneur has used them.

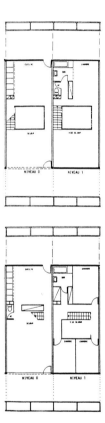

Plan of the duplex flats in the Nemausus block in Nîmes, 1985

Interior of a duplex flat in the
Nemausus block in Nîmes, 1985
Overleaf: external view of the
Nemausus block in Nîmes, 1985

Duodah College in Nîmes (1985)

Another project in Nîmes: converting old buildings into a technical college. I played on an aesthetic reference as a tribute to the artist Yves Klein: marks made in his Yves Klein blue, gold leaf on the steel-work, blow-torched screens...

Views, internal and external, of
Duodah College in Nîmes, 1985

Gymnasium in Nîmes (1986)

Another project in Nîmes, a gymnasium I decided to
daub as though to camouflage it from the neighbours.
Then the patina did its job and made the building look
"acceptable."

Detail of a facade of the
Gymnasium in Nîmes, 1986

CLMBBDO Publicity Agency (1994)

Philippe Michel had a vision of a post-industrial society preparing for a "civilization of the person." The building he commissioned me to create for the new CLMBBDO agency was to incorporate this dimension. For the site on Ile Saint Germain near Paris, I proposed an ageless industrial building that would merge with its surroundings. The unexpected death of Philippe Michel meant he was unable to see the finished building.

Built near a branch of the Seine and its barges, the agency is situated on a lake in which a few blue and green ducks swim: its rough-finish paintwork makes it look corrugated, like a metaphor of an oyster. The roof folds open (a legacy of the Mercedes 300 SL with its butterfly-wing doors) and the interior is smooth, with a pearly shine, the panels covered with holographic paper.

The building is arranged round a huge central space, both a working area and an exhibition area. The offices distributed along the corridors are no longer the obligatory workplace because everyone has a mobile phone. So the designers and copywriters are free to use either the large red armchairs in the central area or the passage-ways where they can sit on the wide parapets. This new method of work suggested a new line in furniture, which was developed with Unifor: secret desks that close up at night like landaus, conference tables made of wood and glass which inscribe themselves in the space, with the red chairs reminiscent of punch-balls.

Interior of an office area, in the foreground one of the typical desks that close up like landaus, executed by Unifor, CLMBBDO Paris, 1994

View from one of the passageways towards the great central hall. Note the pearl-like sheen of the ceiling and the cushioned parapets along the passageways. CLMBBDO Paris, 1994
Below: sectional plan of the building, CLMBBDO Paris, 1994
Overleaf: external, street view of the CLMBBDO Publicity Agency building, CLMBBDO Paris, 1994

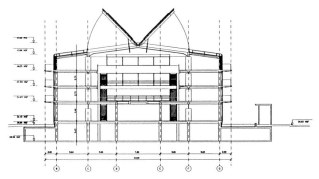

CLM/BBDO

2 allée
des Moulineaux

Club Renault Canal-Boat (1982)

Another example of a rough, industrial exterior contrasting with a sophisticated interior. Renault organized a competition to convert a canal-boat into a club for press conferences. That was no reason to turn it into a kind of pleasure-boat. So I retained the external elements that identified it as a canal-boat with its entirely black and yellow hatchways, the colours of Renault. The interior is treated like the inside of a luxury ship, varnished wooden panels and smooth reddish leather in modules of the same dimensions as the hull-plates.

Internal view of the Club
Renault canal-boat, Paris, 1982

Luxury Director's Office (1989)

An exercise in luxury and sophistication for a director who wanted to retain his own furniture. I merely changed the leather to give it exactly the same colour as the pear-tree wood of the floor, chequered with an artificial white marble from Japan. Storage units at the base of the walls serve as stands for the collector's paintings and objects.

Internal views of the luxury director's office, 1989

Theatre in Belfort (1980)

A 19th-century theatre converted in the nineteen thirties to include extensions for the fire-brigade and a social security office. I wanted to draw a clear distinction between the original building and the extensions. Inside the theatre, with the help of the American artist Gary Glaser, I went to extremes with the decor, the refinement of detail, materials and colours. I retained the traces of the additions in the most brutal and direct manner by scraping the deteriorating plaster and sealing the rough-cast, to the great scandal of the French superintendent for buildings. The facade overlooking the river is a vertical section, as though sliced by a guillotine, with a metal and glass grid.

Internal view of the ballet rehearsal room in Belfort Theatre, 1980

Detail of the facade of Belfort
Theatre on which the American
artist Gary Glaser also worked,
1980

Overall view of Belfort Theatre
towards the river, 1980

Tête Défense (1982)

I have been told that I am obsessed with grids. For the Tête Défense competition which has produced the existing Arche de La Défense, I had submitted a project entitled "Squaring the Horizon." I wanted to frame the perpetually changing sky like a work of art. I was inspired by the process used in classical art, in which a grid can be seen on unfinished paintings, which is an enlargement of the cartoon used as the model; it is a 1 to 10 grid system, which made it easier for the painter to move from the cartoon to the canvas. For this project, I wanted to create the opposite of a perspective: the building seemed to inscribe itself on the paper in the same sense as a sunset and therefore to follow a mathematical sunset. As the spectator approached the building, the lines of the grid would blur like bad print. Once inside, it would look like a Sol LeWitt work, with the grid going off into all three dimensions. As it ascended, the building dematerialized. This 1982 project was my first approach towards what was to be called the aesthetic of dematerialization. Since man has existed, he has fought against matter and attempted to dominate it. This effect of ascent and the gradual dissipation of matter is a process I have used several times, especially for the Tour Sans Fin that would have been situated on the neighbouring site. This aesthetic of the grid, of impregnation and dematerialization through light, is a major concern of mine and I think it also reflects the trend of contemporary research.

Detail of the light-weight,
dissolving structure towards the
top of the building designed for
the Tête Défense competition,
photo of the small-scale model,
1982
Overleaf: photo of the small-scale model for the Tête
Défense competition project,
1982

Cartier Raspail (1993)

The immaterial caught in a grid is the theme of the Cartier Foundation building in Boulevard Raspail. The site is marked by its recent past, with the American centre, and by its more distant past, for the French poet Chateaubriand lived there in the 19th century and planted a cedar tree there. Today that tree is a real historical monument. That is why the architecture endeavours to emphasize it, to frame it. Large glass screens reflect the alignment of the apartment blocks on Boulevard Raspail and give a view of the entire park. It was a delicate project and because of local associations all the trees had to be preserved. Building permission was initially refused. I was told that contemporary architecture would never be accepted. It was, because we held meetings and managed to carry through our ideas about transparency and the effects of matter and its dissolution. For example, the parapet at the top of the building is a three-meter-high glass section through which the entire sky can be seen. The

Detail of the interior of an exhibition hall in the Cartier Foundation building in Paris, 1993

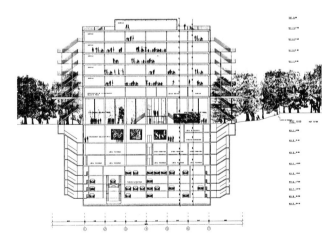

Cross-sectional view of the Cartier Foundation building in Paris, 1993

three successive levels of glass that make up the building convey a sense of ambiguity between the real and the virtual. You never know whether the tree is outside or inside or whether it is a reflection. These are the kind of games that interest the architect or designer.

Inside the office block everything seems evanescent. The partitions are made of three layers of glass, the middle one sand-blasted. The people look like moving and changing shadows depending on the time of day. The Cartier Foundation building is also a fight against matter: the 42-cm-thick floor slabs have a 16-meter span. They contain all the technical equipment. Not a single beam or duct is visible. Everything is smooth.

There is as little furniture as possible, hence its name "Less": desks with thin working tops, pivoting storage units in the form of a totem, a very simple block of drawers and a pull-out computer shelf, partitions free of furniture and the reflection of the furniture in the glass...

Internal view of the offices with the "Less" furniture made by Unifor for the Cartier Foundation building in Paris, 1993
Overleaf: view towards Boulevard Raspail of the Cartier Foundation building in Paris, 1993

French Pavilion
at the Venice Biennale (1990)

This was the prize-winning project for a competition. The French commissioner of the Biennale, Jean Louis Froment, wanted the French Pavilion converted because it was not at all suited to its purpose. That meant modifying and reconstructing it in two stages given the time-scales imposed by Italian law.

Initially, and in order to circumvent the law, which imposed rigorously similar volumetrics, I intended to empty the building and insert a cube. In the second stage I would have duplicated this cube and a 45° rotation would have positioned the pavilion parallel to the canal. Large doors would have opened onto the river bank. All the elements would have been modular. A large roof-light could be closed inside when needed. The pavilion offered maximum flexibility for temporary exhibitions.

Model of the design for the new
French Pavilion of the Venice
Biennale, 1990

Palace of the Cinema in Venice (1990)

Another Venetian project, the palazzo of the Venice film festival on the Lido. The thirties building had been preserved. I inverted the entrance to give access from the lagoon, with a kind of grand staircase below the existing auditorium and a ceiling fresco telling the history of the cinema. The auditorium had a large window framing San Marco in the distance, a window which would be covered up by the screen when the film began. The whole thing was covered by a vast roof in the form of a belvedere overlooking both the Lido and the lagoon towards the town.

Internal view of the cinema auditorium designed for the new Palace of the Cinema competition in Venice. Under the proposed project, until films were shown the screen would be raised, giving a wide view over San Marco and Venice, 1990
Perspective views by A. Buonomo

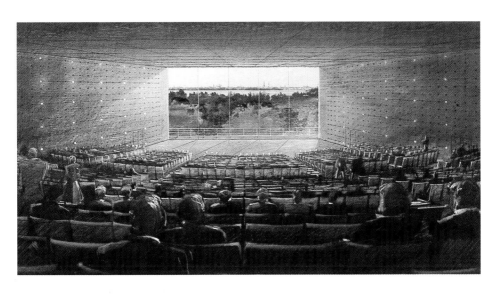

Lannaud Génoscope (1994)

Another belvedere, overlooking the valleyed landscape of the Limousin. It is the home of the Limousin cow and a hymn to the species, the glory of its race, a western architecture entirely in weathered wood gently poised on the site and designed very simply. A miracle of economy too...

View of the Lannaud Génoscope in the rolling countryside of the Limousin, 1994

Detail of a terrace of the
Lannaud Génoscope with
the typical weathered wood
cladding, 1994

Hotel Saint James in Bouliac (1989)

Rural architecture in a village on a hill overlooking the Garonne river and Bordeaux in the distance, a typically French village with its little church and steeple. This hotel is my idea of four-star luxury. First I wanted these buildings to intrude as little as possible into the environment. That is why I gave them the silhouette and colour of the local tobacco hangars: this covering is not corten, it is genuine rusty metal which will gradually acquire a lacy effect. The colour is orange with the kind of grain produced by its cryptogams and fungus, the colour of the sun.

View from one of the rooms in the Hotel Saint James near Bordeaux, 1989

Here we worked as designers: the restaurant chairs are as comfortable as cushions and the covers are removable so that they are always clean. In the rooms, the beds are high in country fashion. From your bed you can see the panorama of Bordeaux. The floors are polished concrete, the walls polished plaster. Everything is kept very simple. Reactions vary. Some customers arrive and say to themselves: hey, they haven't put the carpets down yet! Some leave saying: I don't want a hotel that looks like a prison from the outside and a hospital inside. Others do not understand how to work the head-rests that can be raised for reading or watching TV in comfort. One customer to whom this had been explained phoned later to say he could not sleep sitting up!

Next door is the restaurant, the Bistroye. It is a free and easy place, a bit noisy. Old parquet flooring, a large old counter and on the walls large luminous boxes with big photos of the place in its original state. It is a place that is looking at itself, rather like the Belfort Theatre, with rough walls and posters hung rather haphazardly.

Close-up view of one of the blocks of the Hotel Saint James near Bordeaux. The buildings are entirely covered in rusty iron grids, 1989
Overleaf: overall view of the blocks which make up the complex of the Hotel Saint James near Bordeaux, 1989

Hotel des Thermes in Dax (1992)

This, on the contrary, is my idea of a popular hotel. Originally, I had asked for a budget for a three-star hotel. I only obtained funding for a two-star hotel. But when the committee that awards the stars came to inspect, it found that the hotel was large and well-finished and that it came up to the requisite standards, so it gave it three stars. The third star must therefore go to the architecture.

The entire facade consists of red-cedarwood slatted shutters. Inside, a large hall, a full-height atrium with plants and palms, a greenhouse protected by wooden slats and a spa pool. Inside the rooms, the shutters filter the light and create pretty effects. I opted for extremely simple furniture: all in white or blue. The lamps are like portable miners' lamps. Behind the bed hangs the kind of linen fabric used by the Quakers.

The interior of the atrium is striped by the light and by ropes, as in a boxing ring, which serve as parapets along the walkways.

The bar is also very simple, enhanced here and there by little pieces of coloured glass.

As you can see, none of these projects have much in common. But you know how I love the particular and seek the appropriate solution to the question put to me.

View of the Hotel des Thermes
in Dax, showing the facade
made up entirely of red-
cedarwood slatted shutters,
1992
Overleaf: interior of the large
atrium with plants and the spa
pool, 1992

Housing in Bezons (1994)

This council housing block in the Paris suburbs is also the first block of a future town centre. I have applied the principles developed in Nemausus and Saint Ouen: maximum surface area, thanks in particular to the addition of a winter garden, and apartments facing two ways.

The aesthetic is spontaneous: a large red courtyard, the asphalt marked out for children's games. According to type, the apartments are in different colours—blue, red, yellow, green—produced by the play of a film of colour applied to the windows, a reference to the legacy of that great architect, Le Corbusier.

View of the internal courtyard
of the council housing block
in Bezons, 1994

View towards the street of the
council housing block in Bezons,
1994

Euralille (1994)

In Lille, the tribute to Le Corbusier is even more open since the block of flats has been christened the Le Corbusier block. Here again, the facade is multicoloured and the glass diffuses a coloured light into the apartments.

Euralille is an enormous project comprising 100,000 square meters of offices and apartments and 100,000 square meters of shops which Rem Koolhaas, who drew up the general plan, commissioned me to design. Protected by a vast sloping roof with ground-lights reminiscent of an airport runway, the shopping centre is lit by large areas of glass. It is rhythmic and characterized by large, gleaming surfaces, holographic materials, lights and luminous, coloured shop signs. The towers rise up from the roofing along the entire length of the building. As in Tokyo and Osaka, they will be surmounted by large luminous signs and programmed signals.

Detail of a facade of the Euralille complex, formed of glass panels screen-printed with large images, 1994
Overleaf: view towards the entrance of the shopping centre in the Euralille complex,1994

Galeries Lafayette, Friedrichstrasse, Berlin (1995)

The same concepts of light, of depth, of stressing the commercial aspect by means of signs, recur in the Galeries Lafayette project in Berlin. The building situated right on the Friedrichstrasse is like a little Berlin island in its proportions. This block is pierced by cones which puncture the offices, with a large central cone descending down to the ground floor in the tradition of the large domed departments stores. At the base, the large cone contrasts with another cone that illuminates the parking lot. It is made of glass like a plate-glass mirror through which the signs can be distinguished and onto which images and light effects are projected.

Night view of the Galeries Lafayette shopping centre in Friedrichstrasse in Berlin, 1995
Overleaf: view from above of the large glass cone that descends right through the Galeries Lafayette building in Friedrichstrasse in Berlin, 1995

Mediapark, Cologne (1991)

Mediapark is a complex of "shell and core" offices, in the sense that we do not yet know who will buy or lease them. It is an office block based on the principles of signs and lights, the facade acting as a screen. Each occupant will put his own mark on it through drawings, photos, his own brand or logo, his presence and his identity. When an occupant leaves, the image he imprinted on the building will leave with him. The image of architecture also changes as life changes.

Night view of the model for the
Mediapark project in Cologne,
1991

Grand Stadium (1994)

This is one of the principles I had applied to the Grand Stadium for the 1998 football world cup in Paris. I would have won the competition except that the prime minister decided otherwise and for obscure reasons wanted the contract split between competitors.

The project was based on the variable geometry of stands, to bring the spectators as close as possible to the sports ground, whatever its configuration, and give them a good view. The roof opened up to light up the grass and let the sun in. The actual ground could be covered by a large panel. One of the stands could be slid further forward to adapt to the smaller area required for sports such as basketball or handball or for shows and concerts.

The facades were faced with a large metal net through which large illuminated photos, icons of the champions, could be seen.

Very close to the stadium was a village under canvas for the sponsors, with shops and an area with a large screen for watching or re-watching the matches. There were numerous signposts, to help people find their way around. Nearby were areas for clubs, gym rooms and outdoor sports areas open to everyone.

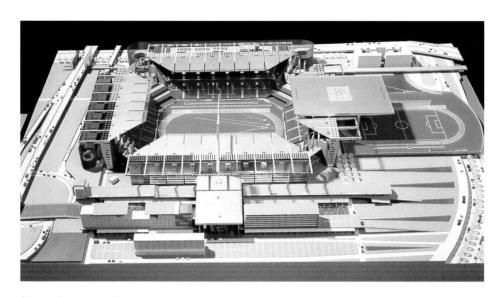

Model of the competition
project for the Grand Stadium
in Paris, 1994. This view shows
the configuration for athletics,
with the steps covered
The model was constructed
by E. Follenfant

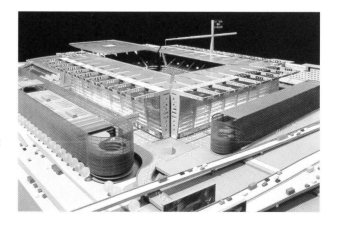

Model of the competition project
for the Grand Stadium in Paris,
1994. General view from
the south-west
The model was constructed
by E. Follenfant

Institut du Monde Arabe, Paris (1987)

I began to consider the question of light at the Institut du Monde Arabe. The theme of the *moucharabieh* or Arab screen is the perforation of a wall by light. This is designed to protect against the climate but is also specific to Arab culture: the wind blows through and women can look out without being seen. True, the problem was different in Paris, where the light is less strong and women do not need to hide themselves. But we wanted to distance ourselves somewhat from the nearby Jussieu University.

Detail of the facade design seen from inside the Institut du Monde Arabe. This clearly shows the decorative effect of the filtered light produced by the camera shutters, 1987

Taking up the themes of geometry and light again, I opted to make the southern facade a wall consisting entirely of camera shutters, so as to create a variable geometry of circles and different kinds of polygons that allowed exactly the required amount of light to penetrate in summer and winter. There are 25,000 camera shutters run by 250 motors linked up to a central computer which decides whether to open or close them depending on the intensity of the outside light. The change of aperture is almost imperceptible, which made some people say the system did not work. So those in charge gave a demonstration of the working of the shutters, which again suggested they did not work... the whole thing became like a Raymond Devos story...

To respond to the sophisticated design of the Arab screens set at intervals in wood and marble, we designed a mechanism inserted between two layers of glass that operates with the delicacy of clockwork, like a grandfather clock. It took two years to perfect the prototype: this was a real design problem, both technically and in terms of manufacture and attention to detail. The ultimate aim was to obtain a specific quality of light. The client, for his part, wondered whether Venetian blinds would not do the same...

The theme of light is also reflected in the stacking of the stairs, the blurring of contours, the reflections and shadows, the superimpositions.

I felt that the north facade, which is not exposed to changes of light, lacked relief, so I attached a silk-screen to it depicting a rather abstract skyline.

We designed the show-cases and modular furniture for the museum. In the case of the auditorium, which had a very small budget, we sought out R-25 seats, which give the impression that the empty room is peopled by extra-terrestrials.

The children's corner was conceived in Oriental colours and motifs. The patio forms the centre of the building, the symbolic centre of Arab culture. It was equipped with a mercury-like fountain... It is framed by walls made of plaques of thin white marble which create the effect of alabaster and diffuse a pale and almost magical light.

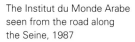

The Institut du Monde Arabe seen from the road along the Seine, 1987

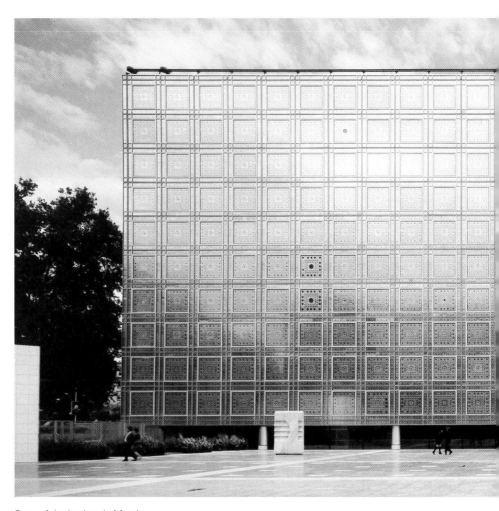

Front of the Institut du Monde
Arabe looking towards the
nearby Jussieu University, 1987

Spa in Vichy (1988)

Diffuse light is also the theme of this spa, which won a competition, although construction was suddenly interrupted. The building, which was to comprise the pools and a three-star hotel, linked up two parks by a large glass and gold vault framing the two landscapes. The shifting light was to pass through walls made of glass slabs as a symbolic reference to the water.

Model of a project for a spa
in Vichy, 1988

Cultural and Congress Centre in Lucerne (1992)

Another example of the principle of framing the landscape applied to the Cultural and Congress Centre in Lucerne, a building on an exceptional site, by the lake facing the town near the old wooden bridge, which had burned down and had been reconstructed. The entire town can be seen from the foyer.

Situated on the corner of the lake, a great wing-like roof which also overhangs the lake shelters the auditorium, a popular music room, a museum, all arranged as though inside a boat-house, of which there are several in the area. The water comes right up to the auditorium and its reflections play on the aluminium false ceiling. The auditorium is surrounded by rooms coloured in a deep and dull crimson lacquer.

Sectional plan of a Cultural
and Congress Centre
in Lucerne, 1992
Drawing by V. Lafont

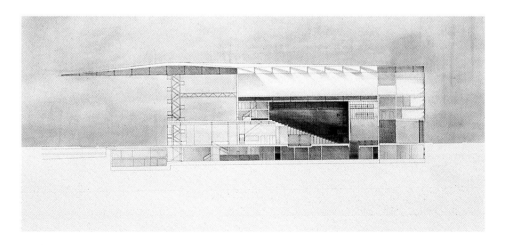

Palace of Congress in Tours (1993)

The plan for this congress centre is analogous to the one in Lucerne: three halls of different sizes under a same roof. The site in the old town faces the station designed by Victor Laloux, architect of the Gare d'Orsay, and adjoins the park of the prefecture. In addition to the congress centre, we designed the surrounding area with the landscape designer Yves Brunier and built a bus station and a small apartment block that also houses the tourist office. Instead of the usual shutters, I protected the southern facade with a large hood.

Front view of the Palace of Congress in Tours, 1993

The three halls are suspended, in order to give a sense of free space and provide side views of the street and the prefecture gardens. This too is a source of plays of light and reflections. The functional blocks are masked by kinds of lanterns made of coloured fluorescent tubes whose volume seems to change depending on the angle of vision. Design, for me, means that too, an attempt at a kind of handwriting and at rendering detail in technical terms.

The furniture consists of the *Elémentaire* series of seats I designed for purposes such as this, when one needs simplicity and can only find objects that are rather too fussy, which I do not think are still suited to our times.

The mayor was afraid I might make the interiors of the halls too grey or black: he wanted colour. In the 2,000-seat auditorium we created colour by projecting photographic films onto alternate white and yellow screens, which gives an effect of movement.

Foreshortened view over
the park from inside the Palace
of Congress in Tours, 1993

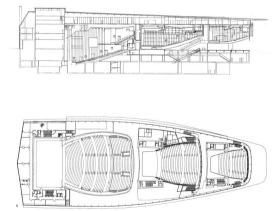

Plan and section of the Palace
of Congress in Tours, 1993

Opera House in Lyons (1993)

The reconstruction of the Lyons Opera House, right in the historic centre of town, caused some controversy. As soon as you site contemporary architecture in a historic centre, you find a resurgence of conservatism. I managed to create three times the original volume, which considerably adapted the roof design, adhering to the spirit and to proportions reminiscent of Italian cities like Florence or Vicenza.

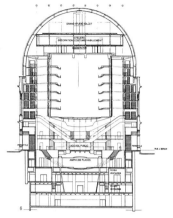

Cross-sectional plan of the Opera House in Lyons, 1993

I wanted to juxtapose two systems in the interior: I kept the original gold in the foyer and treated all the new floors in black granite, polished like a mirror. When you enter the auditorium, you find yourself under the black dome of a hall whose form is reminiscent of a grand piano and which reflects every light. In the black there are red reflections, from the entrance lights to the hall but also from the lights outside, which some of the inhabitants of Lyons see as rather "brothel-like" because the town used to have a red-light area, although I find this criticism a little misplaced in relation to the Opera's repertoire.

Some of the themes of this project can also be found in my project for the Tokyo Opera House: the moving curtain, the gilt panels shining in the dark, the optic fibres, the small candles shining on every spectator's face like the light in Kubrick's film *Barry Lindon*. The gold in the Italian auditorium is the spectators themselves. This multitude of little candles is also a reference to a Lyonnais tradition of placing candles on the window-sills in December.

The seats in the auditorium are original designs. They were specially produced for the Opera by the Tigress firm.

Under the glass double vault of the roof is the dancers' practice room, which looks out over the roofs of the town and the town hall designed by Mansart. At night the dancers' silhouettes are visible through the curve of the glass.

I wanted the Opera House to seem like a beating heart and asked the artist Yann Kersalé to programme a kind of pulsating light effect for the building as a reference to the life within it. When performances are taking place and the House is full, it pulsates and everything becomes brighter. When the audience is small, the light is like the embers of a fire, guarded by the nine muses, who are also red.

Side view of the Opera House in Lyons from the square, 1993
Front view of the Opera House at night during a performance, 1993

Tour Sans Fin at La Défense (1989)

All these plays on matter and light are combined in the Tour Sans Fin. The site abuts the Arche de La Défense. Spreckelsen had hoped to see a minaret near his arch. I do not know if he expected it to be so high.

This project won an international competition. It is meant to be the symbol of an era, of a town, of a business area which claims to be the most powerful in Europe and yet does not even have a church spire.

This is not an apologia to urbanism in vertical form but rather the spire of a Gothic cathedral which narrows until it dissolves into the sky.

This sense of dissolution is produced by the material, black granite rising from the crater, which turns into dark grey, then lighter, with the silk-screened glass becoming increasingly dense and reflective; the top is a simple glass cylinder on two levels without any metal structure. At the very top it is invisible.

On a metaphorical level, this tower forms a link between earth and the cosmos and plays on the continuous effects of light and matter. Here too Yann Kersalé has programmed constantly changing night lights.

Model of the Tour Sans Fin at La Défense, 1989
Below: sectional plan of the Tour Sans Fin at La Défense, 1989

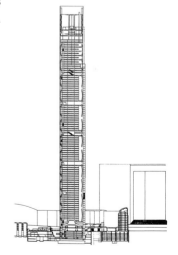

Photomontage showing the site
of the Tour Sans Fin beside
the Arche de La Défense
in Paris, 1989

To return to design, you can see that I have created contradictory objects that reflect personal experiences: the "Milana" chair is an affectionate and slightly ironic re-reading of Mies van der Rohe's "Barcelona"; the "Profil" sofa harks back to a personal event. But these experiences are always linked to plays of matter and light, reinterpreting themes each of which corresponds to a particular purpose and place.

I demand this identity of every creation, this sense of the particular born of the encounter with man. I demand of design the capacity to go to different places and survive in time. I demand of architecture the ability, in inertia, to capture the forces of its time.